Bilingual Edition

LET'S LOOK AT FEELINGS™

Edición Bilingüe

What I Look Like When I Am Confused

Cómo me veo cuando estoy confundido

Joanne Randolph
Traducción al español:
María Cristina Brusca

The Rosen Publishing Group's
PowerStart Press™ & **Editorial Buenas Letras**™
New York

Published in 2004 by The Rosen Publishing Group, Inc.
29 East 21st Street, New York, NY 10010

First Edition

Book Design: Kim Sonsky
Photo Credits: All photos by Maura B. McConnell.

Library of Congress Cataloging-in-Publication Data

Randolph, Joanne.
[What I look like when I am confused. Spanish & English]
What I look like when I am confused = Cómo me veo cuando estoy confundido / Joanne Randolph ; translated by María Cristina Brusca.—1st ed.
     p. cm.— (Let's look at feelings)
Summary: Describes how the parts of the face look when a person is confused.
Spanish and English.
Includes bibliographical references and index.
ISBN 1-4042-7510-X (library binding)
1. Human information processing in children—Juvenile literature. 2.Perception in children—Juvenile literature. [1. Perception. 2. Miscommunication. 3. Facial expression. 4. Emotions. 5. Spanish language material—Bilingual.]
I. Title: Cómo me veo cuando estoy confundido. II. Title. III. Series.
BF723.I63R3618 2004
152.4–dc21

                                                                          2003009128

Manufactured in the United States of America

Due to the changing nature of Internet links, PowerStart Press has developed an online list of Web sites related to the subject of this book. This site is updated regularly. Please use this link to access the list:

http://www.buenasletraslinks.com/llafe/confundido

Contents

Contenido

I am confused.

Estoy confundido.

When I am confused my
eyes look up.

Cuando estoy confundido,
mis ojos miran hacia arriba.

7

When I am confused my eyes look to the side.

Cuando estoy confundida, mis ojos miran a un costado.

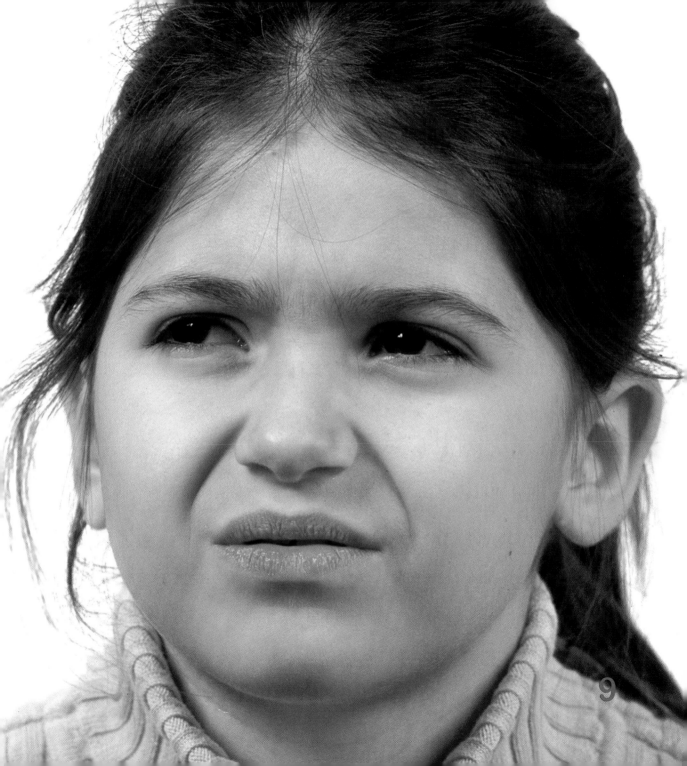

I get lines on my nose
when I am confused.

Cuando estoy confundida,
se forman líneas en mi nariz.

When I am confused
my cheeks get round.

Cuando estoy confundida,
mis mejillas se redondean.

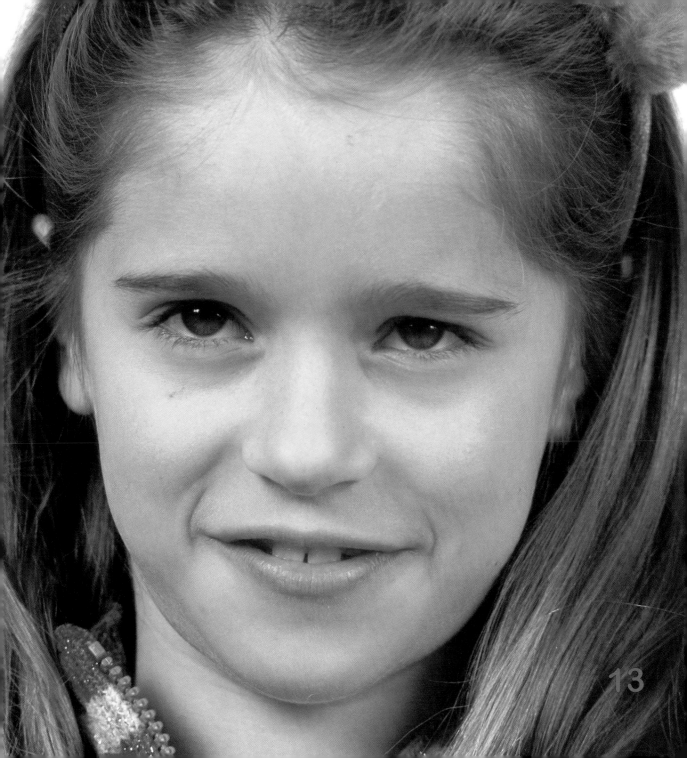

13

I get lines by my mouth
when I am confused.

_____

Se forman líneas junto
a mi boca, cuando
estoy confundido.

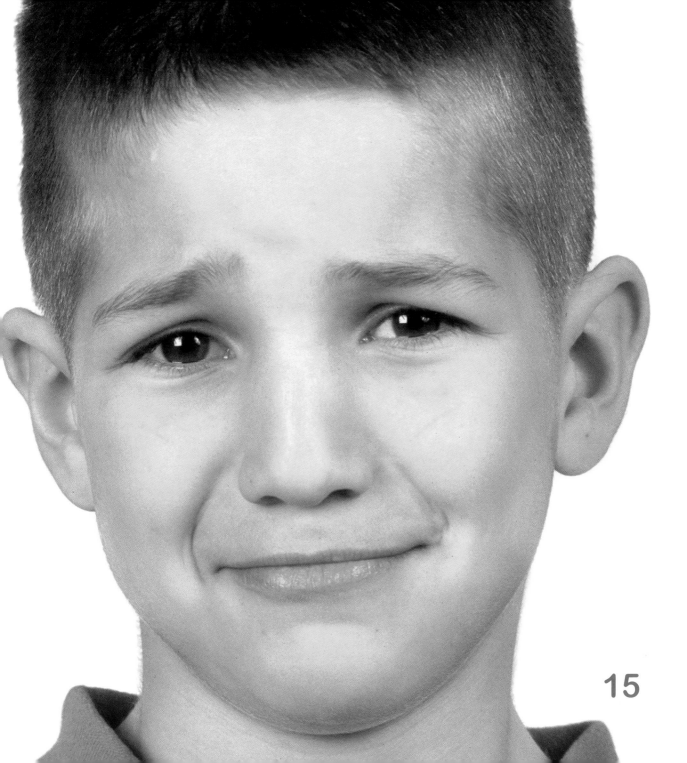

15

When I am confused
my mouth opens.

Cuando estoy confundida,
mi boca se abre.

My mouth moves to the side when I am confused.

Mi boca se mueve hacia un costado, cuando estoy confundida.

19

When I am confused my chin drops down.

Cuando estoy confundido, mi mentón se baja.

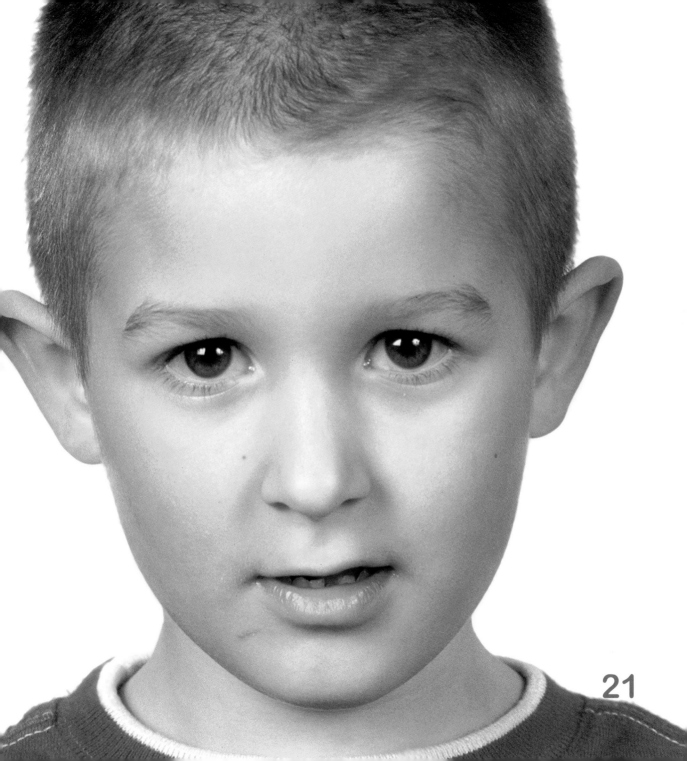

21

This is what I look like
when I am confused.

Así me veo cuando
estoy confundida.

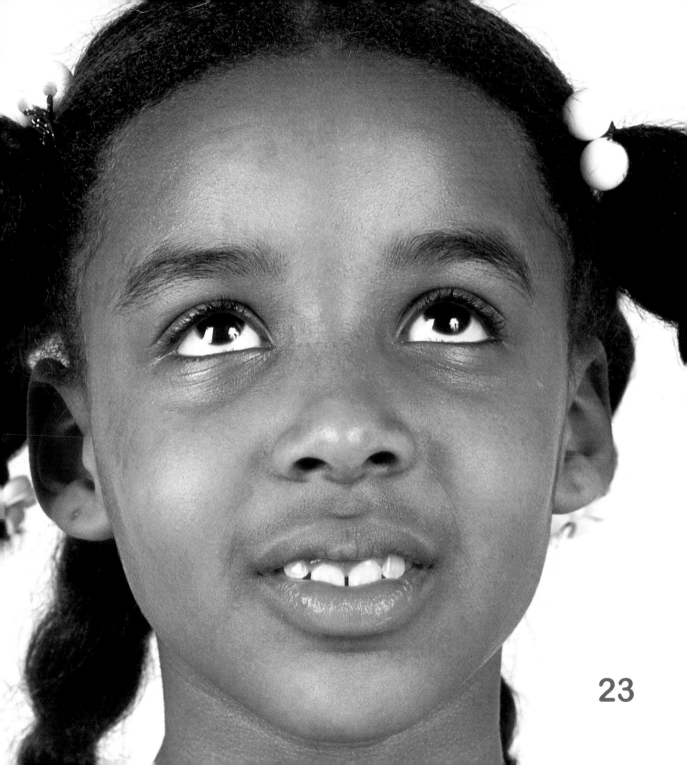

23

Words to Know
Palabras que debes saber

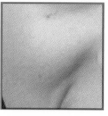

cheek
mejilla

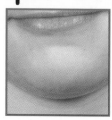

chin
mentón

eye
ojo

mouth
boca

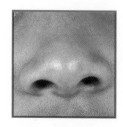

nose
nariz